FAMILY FUN

- Help your child think of important dates, such as holidays and birthdays. Talk about the season in which each occurs. Divide a sheet of paper into four columns with *WINTER, SPRING, SUMMER,* and *FALL* as the headings. Write the special days under the appropriate column.

- Help your child make seasonal collages by cutting out pictures depicting the seasons from old magazines. Have your child paste the pictures of each season on a separate sheet of paper, then display the appropriate picture each season.

READ MORE ABOUT IT

- *Why Do Leaves Change Color?*
- *Why Do Animals Sleep Through Winter?*
- *Why Do Birds Fly South?*

WEEKLY READER BOOKS presents

What Are Seasons?

A **Just Ask**™ Book

Hi, my name is Christopher!

by Chris Arvetis
and Carole Palmer

illustrated by
James Buckley

FIELD PUBLICATIONS
MIDDLETOWN, CT.

Christopher, take the pumpkin and stand there.

The season is spring.

Hold the earth so that the North Pole tilts this way.

The earth tilts as it travels around the sun.

So different places receive different amounts of sunlight during the year.

That makes the seasons.

Now, walk around the sun.
Follow the rope.
Stop!
You are now in the summer season.
It is hot because our part of the earth is tilted even more **toward** the sun.
The sunlight warms the air and land around us.

Walk on.

Now it is winter.

Why?

The earth is tilted **farther away** from the sun.

We get less sunlight during the winter season.

Days are short.

There is little time for the sunlight to warm the earth.

The earth's trip around the sun takes one year. That's 365 days.

Let's start at spring again.

Think about spring.

Spring begins around March 20th each year.

Spring means it begins to get warmer— rain and umbrellas, plants begin to grow, baseball season is here.

The next season is fall.
It is also called autumn.
Fall begins around
September 22nd.
Fall means cooler weather
and shorter days—
leaves turning color
and falling, school has
started, football season
is here.

The next season is winter. Winter begins about December 21st.

Winter means cold weather and snow— scarfs and mittens, skating and sleds, basketball and hockey.

And those are the four seasons for many places on earth.
There are some that get more sunlight all year long.
Those places are very hot.
Others get less sunlight.
Those places have ice and snow all year long.